Masterbuilt Smoker Cookbook #2020

Simple, Quick and Delicious Masterbuilt Smoker Recipes for Happy and Leisure Living (The Complete Masterbuilt Electric Smoker Cookbook)

Rager Prass

© Copyright 2019 Rager Prass - All Rights Reserved.

In no way is it legal to reproduce, duplicate, or transmit any part of this document by either electronic means or in printed format. Recording of this publication is strictly prohibited, and any storage of this material is not allowed unless with written permission from the publisher. All rights reserved.

The information provided herein is stated to be truthful and consistent, in that any liability, regarding inattention or otherwise, by any usage or abuse of any policies, processes, or directions contained within is the solitary and complete responsibility of the recipient reader. Under no circumstances will any legal liability or blame be held against the publisher for any reparation, damages, or monetary loss due to the information herein, either directly or indirectly.

Respective authors own all copyrights not held by the publisher.

Legal Notice:

This book is copyright protected. This is only for personal use. You cannot amend, distribute, sell, use, quote or paraphrase any part of the content within this book without the consent of the author or copyright owner. Legal action will be pursued if this is breached.

Disclaimer Notice:

Please note the information contained within this document is for educational and entertainment purposes only. Every attempt has been made to provide accurate, up-to-date and reliable, complete information. No warranties of any kind are expressed or implied. Readers acknowledge that the author is not engaging in the rendering of legal, financial, medical or professional advice.

By reading this document, the reader agrees that under no circumstances are we responsible for any losses, direct or indirect, which are incurred as a result of the use of information contained within this document, including, but not limited to, errors, omissions, or inaccuracies.

Table of contents

Introduction 7
Chapter 1: History of Masterbuilt Electric Smoker 8
Chapter 2: Getting to Know Masterbuilt 9
Chapter 3: How an Electric Smoker Works 10
Chapter 4: Benefits of Smoker 12
Chapter5: Tips 14
Chapter 6: FAQ 16
Chapter 7: Poultry 18
    Flavorful Orange Chicken 18
    Mexican Chicken 20
    Chipotle Chicken 22
    Harissa Chicken Wings 23
    Turkey Wings 24
    BBQ Chicken Legs 25
    Easy Cajun Chicken 26
    Flavorful & Moist Turkey Breast 27
    Smoked Chicken Thighs 28
    Smoked Turkey 29
    Flavorful Chicken Drumsticks 30
    Simple BBQ Chicken Wings 31
    Tender & Juicy Chicken Breast 32
    Juicy Turkey Breast 34
    Simple Jerk Chicken 35
Chapter 8: Fish & Seafood 36
    Fresh Smoked Salmon 36
    Cajun Shrimp 37

Smoked Scallops 38

Smoked Trout Fillets 39

Smoked Salmon 40

Greek Shrimp 41

Lobster Tails 42

Lemon Shrimp 43

Chapter 9: Pork 44

Tender & Juicy Pork Chops 44

Perfect Baby Back Ribs 46

Smoked Pork Belly 48

Easy Pork Steaks 49

Pulled Pork 50

Pork Tenderloin 52

BBQ Shredded Pork 53

Honey Butter Ribs 54

Easy Smoked Pork Tenderloin 56

Delicious Pork Chops 57

Chapter 10: Beef 58

Cajun Seasoned Beef Brisket 58

Meatloaf 60

Garlic Herb Beef Roast 61

Chuck Roast 62

Juicy Beef Ribs 63

Meatballs 64

Easy Beef Patties 65

Tip Roast 66

Flavorful Beef Tenderloin 67

Perfect Beef Brisket 68

Chapter 11: Lamb 69

Leg of Lamb 69

Olive Wood Smoked Lamb 70

Rack of Lamb 71

Smoked Lamb Chops 73

Dijon Rack of Lambs 74

Smoked Leg of Lamb 76

Delicious Lamb Rack 77

BBQ Smoked Lamb 78

Garlickey Leg of Lamb 79

Indian Spiced Lamb 80

Chapter 12: Game Recipes 82

Easy Smoked Cornish Hens 82

Flavorful Cornish Hen 83

Orange Glazed Cornish Hens 84

Herb Butter Cornish Hens 86

Orange Stuff Cornish Hens 87

Herbed Cornish Hens 88

Delicious Cornish Game Hens 89

Smoked Vension Tenderloins 90

BBQ Cornish Hens 92

Asian Smoked Cornish Hen 93

Simple Smoked Cornish Hens 94

Easy & Flavorful Cornish Hens 95

Chapter 13: Sides 96

Smoked Olives & Cherry Tomatoes 96

Smoked Shrimp Skewers 97
Beef Bites 98
Smoked Green Beans 99
Sweet & Smoky Ketchup 100
Baked Beans 101
Smoked Mac & Cheese 102
Smoked Asparagus 103
Simple Smoked Scallops 104
Smoked Italian Meatballs 105
Conclusion 106

Introduction

Smoking food is one of the preferred ways to preserve food for a long time. Smoking food not just used to preserve the food it helps to cook your food in a natural way. It adds delicious flavors into your food and also give nice texture over it. Smoking does not only make delicious food it also helps to cook food into large quantities at a time.

In this book we have to introduce one of the most interesting cooking methods knows as smoking food. Smoking food is one of the traditional methods to cook food with smoke. Smoke gives woody flavor to your food. Smokers are one of the advanced machines used to smoke foods. You can smoke any type of meat into smoker. Traditional smokers are run on charcoal and propane. New smokers are runs on electricity they use the constant and clean source of energy to cook and smoke your food. In this book, we have to learn about Masterbuilt electric smoker. This step by step guide helps you to know more about Masterbuilt electric smoker from its history to make a delicious recipe. Using this book, you can easily understand the various benefits of the electric smoker with some useful tips and tricks.

If you are one of that people who love home-made Smokey food without doing extra efforts, then you have to purchase the right book. Each chapter in this book has a distinct purpose. The first chapter tells you the history of Masterbuilt electric smoker. The second chapter introduces you with the machine. The third chapter gives you a brief knowledge about how to use an electric smoker. The last chapter will provide you with the secret of smoking food enjoying healthy and delicious recipes. If you are new to smoking, then I will highly recommend this brief guide of smoking.

My goal here is to provide all brief information about the Masterbuilt electric smoker with some useful tips and tricks. There are plenty of books on this subject are available in the market thanks for choosing this one.

Chapter 1: History of Masterbuilt Electric Smoker

Smoking Food is one of the techniques introduced our ancestors when they newly introduce fire. They cook their food directly over an open fire; smoking food adds flavors into meats. These smoking food techniques are used in smokers and these smokers are run on charcoal and propane. Propane smokers are very messy and expensive. Smoking techniques are changes during the time period with the help of advanced equipment's. Here we have talked about one of the recent smokers popularly known as Masterbuilt electric smoker.

Masterbuilt is started in 1973 to manufacture electric smokers. Masterbuilt electric smokers are somewhat similar like a traditional smoker. They are energy efficient electric smokers used wood chips for fast heating mechanism. Dowson Mclemore the owner of Masterbuilt working on the mechanism and design of electric smokers. They turn their welding hobby into his family business and develop energy-efficient electric smoker. There are so many electric smokers made by Masterbuilt these smokers are safe and reliable. They come with new features and techniques to help you with your smoking activities. They have developed a long-standing brand in the category of the electric smoker. They make a quality product from their hard work.

Chapter 2: Getting to Know Masterbuilt

Masterbuilt is the leading name in smoker manufacturer today. Smoker adds flavors into your cuts and meats. Smoking food is one of the techniques to preserve your food. It gives nice color and texture to your food and also adds aromas, smoky flavors to improve the taste of your food. It burns wood pellets to smoke your food. These wood pellets are made with the help of the hardwood sawdust. The wood pellets are available in the market with different flavors like hickory, apple, cherry, maple, oak, peach, mesquite, bourbon, alder, pecan, etc. to make your own flavor you can mix these wood pellets. Wood pallets help to cook your food easy and faster way.

Masterbuilt electric smoker allows you to grills and smokes different types of food like pork hinds, whole chicken, sausage, ribs, turkeys and vegetables. Masterbuilt provides a good cooking tool for its consumers. It comes with a digital control panel where you can set temperature and cooking time for your food. These smokers also come with smoking racks which helps you to cook a large quantity of food at a time. Smoking racks come with chrome coating, for smoke control adjustable air damper are present at the top side. It comes with a fully insulated body and side wood chip loading system. Latest models of Masterbuilt electric smoker come with digital electric with Bluetooth connectivity. The current smokers with Bluetooth connectivity come with a built-in meat thermometer. This will help you to monitor the internal temperature of your meat. You can easily adjust temperature and time through your Smartphone.

Chapter 3: How an Electric Smoker Works

In this chapter, we have learned step by step process how the electric smoker works.

- Season Smoker

If your smoker is new then you have to need to season your smoker before first use. Seasoning electric smoker means burning off any residue left over during the manufacturing process like dust particles and machine oils. Start seasoning with placing the wood chip pan and water pan into smoker box at their place. Then close the main door and plug the power cord in to switch and on the smoker. Then set the temperature at 275-degree F for at least 2 hours. After 1-hour completions pulls the wood chip pan and add half portion of chips into the pan and set pan at its position. Wait until the smoking time is over. After completion of smoking time power off the smoker and let it cool down completely. Now the smoker is ready for first use.

- Prepare your smoker

First, get the wood chip from the market or you can buy it from the online store. These wood chips are coming with different flavors like apple, plum, cherry, peach, mesquite, bourbon, alder, pecan, etc. you just choose flavor as per your taste. A smoker needs near about 4 cups of wood chips every 4 to 5 hours of use. Before start cooking store enough amount of wood chips.

- Preheat your Smoker

Commonly electric smoker takes 30 to 45 minutes to heat up from cold. Before turning on your electric smoker you need to add a cup of wood chips into the chip pan. Then turn your smoker on and set the desired temperature and time for preheating smoker. If the smoker is unable to produce required smoke, then you need to add more wood chips into chip pan. More smoke will help to add more flavor into your meat. Once your smoker is preheated then adjust the temperature at 225-degree F because this is one of the ideal temperatures to cook most types of meats.

- Add your food into electric smoker

After finishing the preheating process add you're prepared or marinade food into the smoker grill.

- Add more wood chips and water into the pan

If you notice that the smoke is not enough then pull the wood chip pan from the smoker and add a cup of the wood chip into wood chip pan. Insert pan inside the smoker this will help to raise the inside temperature and your meat will have smoked perfectly.

- Turn off smoker

When your food smoked perfectly then turns off the smoker. Then remove the food from the smoker and transfer it into serving plate to rest for some time before serve. After smoker is cool down then clean it properly for the next dish.

Chapter 4: Benefits of Smoker

- Easy to operate

Electric smokers are easy to operate you just need to turn on smoker then fill the wood chips into wood chip pan and fill the water into a water tray. Preheat the smoker at desire temperature then loaded smoker with food. After loading food into smoker set the cooking time and temperature and waits until the food is cooked. Most of the advanced smokers are equipped with Bluetooth technology. You can operate this machine remotely. You can set temperature and timing and also check the internal temperature of your meat. You can operate your smoker with the help of your Smartphone device.

- Safe to use

Masterbuilt electric smokers are safe and healthy to use compare to the other smokers it does not emits any harmful pollutants into the surrounding air. This type of smoker is safe for use to compare to other smokers like propane.

- Digital controller

Most of the Masterbuilt electric smokers are equipped with a digital controller. You can easily set the temperature and cooking time over it. If the temperature increases from the pre-set setting the smoker circuit are broken down automatically until the temperature drops down.

- Save electricity

Masterbuilt electric smoker requires less electricity compared to any other electric smoker. Masterbuilt electric smoker is made of thick steel due to this they absorb heat and equally redistribute into the cooking chamber. This will help to cook your food evenly.

- Sturdy

Masterbuilt electric smoker comes with the support of thick steel legs. Smoker cabinet is sturdy and well-constructed made up of high gauge stainless steel. You can cook your meat for overnight without the worry of messing your food by any pet at your home.

- Mess-free cooking

Electric smoker is not messy compared to other smoker run on propane. There is no need to clean charcoal ash and no need to change propane tank. It just runs on a clean energy source. This will help you to cook your food without any mess.

- Average cost

Masterbuilt electric smoker gives you well-equipped smoker into average price point. It doesn't break down your bank account. The average price of this smoker is in the range of $100 to $400.

- Does not need constant supervision

Other smokers like propane and charcoal smoker need constant monitoring during the cooking process is not interrupted due to lack of fuel. The electric smoker does not need constant monitoring during the cooking process because it has a constant electricity supply. During cooking, you can do your other activities. After finishing cooking time just serve and enjoy your meal.

Chapter5: Tips

Masterbuilt electric smoker is very easy to use and doesn't require any special skill to use here in this chapter we have seen some useful tips about Masterbuilt electric smoker.

- Pre-season your smoker before using it for the first time. Pre seasoning process means burning of any dust particles, residues, and machine oil leftover during the manufacturer process.
- Always preheat your electric smoker before inserting food inside the smoker. Preheating helps to cook your food by perfection. Before using smoker preheat it at 230-degree F temperature for 30 to 40 minutes. Monitor thermometer to know that the smoker reaches the desired temperature.
- Choose the right woodchips because some woodchips are producing unhealthy gas which is harmful to your health. It is recommended to use hardwood chips which are available many flavors in the market like apple, hickory, cherry, maple, peach, mesquite, pecan, etc. use these chips to smoking food into the electric smoker.
- To save clean-up time use foil over grill rack this will reduce your clean-up work. you can also use foil to cover the drip pan and heat deflector pan.
- Don't over smoke your food a little smoke adds flavors into your food. When you cook chicken then you have to add only one cup of wood chips to get a decent flavor to your dish.
- When you smoke chicken the choose hotter temperature setting. Smoke your chicken at 275-degree F temperature for 1 ½ to 2 hours. Check the internal temperature of the chicken with the help of thermostat make sure internal temperature reaches 165-degree F. this kind of chicken is safe to eat.
- While using Masterbuilt electric smoker it is better to open vent fully when you smoke your meat. An open vent will help you to avoid the creosote building risk on your meat. A small amount of creosote adds taste into your food but the layer of creosote makes your food taste terrible. The vent is only close when you are finishing the smoking process. This will increase the internal temperature of the smoker.
- Use brine solution to soak your meat before cooking this will make your meat delicious, tenderized and flavorful. To prepare brine solution by mixing spices and

salt into water then soak your meat in this solution for at least 4 hours. You can also soak it overnight. Remember that the meat is completely immersed in the brine solution.

- Clean your Masterbuilt smoker regularly to achieve the best results. Always clean grease and leftover oil from your electric smoker before second use. If you leave it too long it is hard to clean-up. Most of the electric smokers come with detachable parts you can easily remove them for cleaning. This will make your cleaning process easy. Instead of cleaning chemicals use vinegar and water mixture for effective cleaning your smoker.

Chapter 6: FAQ

- Should I have used wet or dry wood chips?

You can use pre-soaked wood chips or dry wood chips. Where pre-soaked (soak approximately 30 minutes) wood chip burns slowly and produces less intense smoke during smoking. On the other side, dry wood chips burn faster and also produce large intense smoke during the smoking process.

- What kind of wood chips used in the smoker?

Use right wood chips because low-quality wood chips produce harmful gases. Always try to use hardwood chips these wood chips are easily available in the market and comes in different flavors like apple, maple, cherry, plum, peach, mesquite, alder, hickory, oak, etc.

- What is the best cleaning method for my smoker?

Cleaning Masterbuilt electric smoker is easy. Take a mixture of 50 percent hot water and 50 percent apple cider vinegar. Fill these mixers into a spray bottle and apply it into a smoker. Clean with the help of a soft sponge. Do not use any harsh chemicals to clean your electrical smoker.

- Can I use my smoker into my car garage?

Smokers need an open place where proper ventilation is available. Do not use smoker into covered areas like garage, kitchen or covered porches. Keep a minimum of 10 feet of distance from any structure and building. Masterbuilt electric smokers are only for outdoor use as you can use it to your home backyard.

- What is pre-season smoker first time?

Pre-season means you have to burn any dust particles, residues, and machine oil leftover during the manufacturing process. You have followed a simple method to pre-seasoning your smoker. Set the water pan without water into its place then set smoker temperature at 275-degree F and run the unit for three hours. When the last hour remains then add one cup of the wood chip into the wood chip tray. After completion of 3 hours' time power off the unit and let it cool down completely. Now your smoker is ready for first use.

- Why some times wood chips not burning?

This is happening due to overloading wood chips into wood chip loader tray or over soaked chips are used. Start your smoker with a smaller quantity of wood chips when the fire going on then add some more chips into wood chip tray.

Chapter 7: Poultry

Flavorful Orange Chicken

Preparation Time: 10 minutes
Cooking Time: 1 hour 30 minutes
Serve: 2

Ingredients:

- 2 chicken quarters, wash & dry with paper towels
- 6 tbsp hot sauce
- 7 tbsp orange marmalade
- For rub:
- ¼ tsp cayenne pepper
- ¼ tsp sweet paprika
- ¼ tsp onion powder
- 1 ½ tsp garlic powder
- 1 ½ tsp thyme
- 1 tbsp chili powder
- 3 tsp paprika
- ½ tsp pepper
- 1 ½ tsp salt

Directions:

1. Preheat the smoker to 275 F.
2. In a small bowl, mix together all rub ingredients.
3. Rub chicken with spice mixture and brush with hot sauce and orange marmalade.
4. Place chicken in the preheated smoker and cook for 1 hour 30 minutes.
5. Serve and enjoy.

Nutritional Value (Amount per Serving):

- Calories 543
- Fat 24 g
- Carbohydrates 60 g
- Sugar 45 g
- Protein 26 g
- Cholesterol 140 mg

Mexican Chicken

Preparation Time: 10 minutes
Cooking Time: 5 hours
Serve: 8

Ingredients:

- 6 lbs whole chicken
- For rub:
- ½ tsp ground cinnamon
- 1 tbsp ground cumin
- 1 tbsp paprika
- 1 ½ tbsp chili powder
- 1 tbsp honey
- 4 garlic cloves, minced
- 1 tbsp olive oil
- 1 tbsp fresh lime juice
- ½ tsp pepper
- 1 tbsp kosher salt

Directions:

1. Preheat the smoker to 225 F using the applewood chips.
2. In a small bowl, mix together all rub ingredients and rub all over the chicken.
3. Place chicken in the smoker and cook for 4-5 hours or until the internal temperature of chicken reaches to 170 F.
4. Slice and serve.

Nutritional Value (Amount per Serving):

- Calories 682
- Fat 27.5 g
- Carbohydrates 4.4 g

- Sugar 2.4 g
- Protein 99 g
- Cholesterol 303 mg

Chipotle Chicken

Preparation Time: 5 minutes
Cooking Time: 3 hours
Serve: 4

Ingredients:

- 4 chicken breasts, skinless and boneless
- 1 1/2 tsp chipotle powder
- 3/4 tsp onion powder
- 1/2 tsp garlic powder
- 1/3 cup maple syrup
- 1/2 tsp pepper
- 1 tsp salt

Directions:

1. Preheat the smoker to 250 F using the applewood chips.
2. Mix together chipotle powder, onion powder, garlic powder, pepper, and salt and rub over chicken breasts.
3. Place chicken in the smoker and smoke for 1 hour.
4. Brush chicken with half maple syrup and smoke for 2 hours more.
5. Slice and serve.

Nutritional Value (Amount per Serving):

- Calories 349
- Fat 10.9 g
- Carbohydrates 18.4 g
- Sugar 15.9 g
- Protein 42.4 g
- Cholesterol 130 mg

Harissa Chicken Wings

Preparation Time: 10 minutes
Cooking Time: 2 hours
Serve: 4

Ingredients:

- 2 lbs chicken wings
- 1 1/2 tbsp harissa paste
- 3/4 tsp garlic powder
- 2 tbsp brown sugar
- 1 tsp salt

Directions:

1. In a large bowl, mix together harissa, garlic powder, sugar, and salt.
2. Add chicken wings to the bowl and coat well.
3. Preheat the smoker to 275 F using the cherry wood chips.
4. Place chicken wings in the smoker and smoke for 2 hours.
5. Serve and enjoy.

Nutritional Value (Amount per Serving):

- Calories 450
- Fat 16.8 g
- Carbohydrates 4.8 g
- Sugar 4.5 g
- Protein 65.7 g
- Cholesterol 202 mg

Turkey Wings

Preparation Time: 10 minutes
Cooking Time: 2 hours
Serve: 4

Ingredients:

- 4 turkey wings
- 1 tbsp sugar
- 2 1/2 tbsp chili powder
- 1 tsp cayenne pepper
- 3/4 tsp garlic powder
- 1 tsp salt

Directions:

1. Mix together chili powder, cayenne pepper, garlic powder, sugar, and salt and rub over turkey wings.
2. Preheat the smoker to 275 F using the applewood chips.
3. Place turkey wings in the smoker and smoke for 2 hours.
4. Serve and enjoy.

Nutritional Value (Amount per Serving):

- Calories 211
- Fat 10.9 g
- Carbohydrates 6.2 g
- Sugar 3.5 g
- Protein 23.7 g
- Cholesterol 0 mg

BBQ Chicken Legs

Preparation Time: 10 minutes
Cooking Time: 1 hour 45 minutes
Serve: 8

Ingredients:

- 14 chicken legs, rinsed and pat dry with paper towels
- 1 3/4 cups BBQ sauce

Directions:

1. Preheat the smoker to 275 F using the applewood chips.
2. Place chicken legs in the smoker and cook for 1 hour 30 minutes.
3. Remove chicken legs from smoker and brush with BBQ sauce.
4. Return chicken legs to the smoker and cook for 15 minutes more or until the internal temperature of chicken reaches to 165 F.
5. Serve and enjoy.

Nutritional Value (Amount per Serving):

- Calories 545
- Fat 27 g
- Carbohydrates 19.8 g
- Sugar 14.3 g
- Protein 51.8 g
- Cholesterol 184 mg

Easy Cajun Chicken

Preparation Time: 10 minutes
Cooking Time: 2 hours
Serve: 2

Ingredients:

- 2 chicken quarters
- 6 tbsp Cajun seasoning

Directions:

1. Preheat the smoker to 275 F using the applewood chips.
2. Rub chicken quarters with Cajun seasoning and place in the smoker and cook for 1-2 hours or until the internal temperature of chicken reaches to 160 F.
3. Remove chicken from the smoker and let sit for 15 minutes.
4. Slice and serve.

Nutritional Value (Amount per Serving):

- Calories 390
- Fat 26 g
- Carbohydrates 15 g
- Sugar 2 g
- Protein 26 g
- Cholesterol 140 mg

Flavorful & Moist Turkey Breast

Preparation Time: 10 minutes
Cooking Time: 3 hours
Serve: 10

Ingredients:

- 3 lbs turkey breast, boneless
- 8 bacon slices
- 2 tsp herb seasoning
- 2 tbsp olive oil
- Pepper
- Salt

Directions:

1. Brush turkey breast with oil and season with herb seasoning, pepper, and salt.
2. Wrap bacon slices around the turkey breast.
3. Preheat the smoker to 250 F using cherry wood chips.
4. Place turkey breast in the smoker and cook for 3-4 hours or until internal temperature reaches to 160 F.
5. Remove bacon slices from turkey breast.
6. Slice turkey breast and serve.

Nutritional Value (Amount per Serving):

- Calories 248
- Fat 11.4 g
- Carbohydrates 6 g
- Sugar 4.8 g
- Protein 28.9 g
- Cholesterol 75 mg

Smoked Chicken Thighs

Preparation Time: 10 minutes
Cooking Time: 3 hours
Serve: 6

Ingredients:

- 2 lbs chicken thighs, bone-in and skin-on
- 1 1/2 tbsp BBQ rub
- 3/4 cup BBQ sauce

Directions:

1. Preheat the smoker to 250 F using the hickory wood chips.
2. Coat chicken with BBQ rub and place into the smoker and smoke for 3 hours or until the internal temperature of chicken reaches to 165 F.
3. Brush chicken with BBQ sauce and smoke for 10 minutes more.
4. Serve and enjoy.

Nutritional Value (Amount per Serving):

- Calories 334
- Fat 11.3 g
- Carbohydrates 11.3 g
- Sugar 8.1 g
- Protein 43.7 g
- Cholesterol 135 mg

Smoked Turkey

Preparation Time: 10 minutes
Cooking Time: 6 hours
Serve: 12

Ingredients:

- 10 lbs whole turkey, remove giblets
- 2 fresh rosemary sprigs
- 1 lemon, quartered
- 1 onion, quartered
- 1/2 cup BBQ rub
- 3 cups chicken stock
- 2 fresh thyme sprigs

Directions:

1. Preheat the smoker to 250 F using the hickory wood chips.
2. Spray foil pan with cooking spray.
3. Place turkey in foil pan.
4. Stuff turkey cavity with herbs, onion, and lemon and tie the turkey legs together using the kitchen twine.
5. Coat turkey with BBQ rub.
6. Place the turkey into the smoker and smoke for 6-7 hours or until the internal temperature of the turkey reaches to 165 F.
7. Remove turkey from the smoker and let it cool for 10 minutes.
8. Slice and serve.

Nutritional Value (Amount per Serving):

- Calories 411
- Fat 3.5 g
- Carbohydrates 1 g
- Sugar 0.6 g
- Protein 77.9 g
- Cholesterol 236 mg

Flavorful Chicken Drumsticks

Preparation Time: 10 minutes
Cooking Time: 2 hours
Serve: 4

Ingredients:

- 10 chicken drumsticks
- 3 garlic cloves, minced
- 3 tbsp olive oil
- 10 bacon slices
- 1 tsp cayenne pepper
- 3 tbsp brown sugar
- 1/3 cup soy sauce

Directions:

1. In a large bowl, mix together soy sauce, cayenne, garlic, oil, and sugar.
2. Add chicken to the bowl and coat well.
3. Cover bowl and place in the refrigerator for 2 hours.
4. Drain chicken drumsticks and wrap bacon slices around each chicken drumstick.
5. Preheat the smoker to 250F using the cherry wood chips.
6. Place chicken drumsticks into the smoker and smoke for 2 hours.
7. Serve and enjoy.

Nutritional Value (Amount per Serving):

- Calories 583
- Fat 37 g
- Carbohydrates 9.9 g
- Sugar 7 g
- Protein 50.8 g
- Cholesterol 153 mg

Simple BBQ Chicken Wings

Preparation Time: 10 minutes
Cooking Time: 2 hours
Serve: 6

Ingredients:

- 3 lbs chicken wings
- 2 tbsp BBQ rub
- 3/4 cup BBQ sauce

Directions:

1. Preheat the smoker to 250F using the hickory wood chips.
2. Rub chicken wings with BBQ rub and place into the smoker and smoke for 2 hours.
3. Transfer chicken wings to a baking tray and brush with BBQ sauce.
4. Broil chicken wings for 3-4 minutes.
5. Serve and enjoy.

Nutritional Value (Amount per Serving):

- Calories 478
- Fat 16.9 g
- Carbohydrates 11.3 g
- Sugar 8.1 g
- Protein 65.6 g
- Cholesterol 202 mg

Tender & Juicy Chicken Breast

Preparation Time: 10 minutes
Cooking Time: 1 hour 30 minutes
Serve: 6

Ingredients:

- 2 lbs chicken breasts, skinless and boneless
- 1 cup BBQ sauce
- For rub:
- 1/8 tsp cayenne
- 1/4 tsp mustard powder
- 1/4 tsp onion powder
- 1/4 tsp garlic powder
- 1/2 tsp paprika
- 1 tsp smoked paprika
- 1 tbsp sugar
- 1/4 tsp pepper
- 1 tsp kosher salt

Directions:

1. Preheat the smoker to 250F using the cherry wood chips.
2. Mix together all rub ingredients and rub over chicken.
3. Place chicken in the smoker and smoke for 1 hour 30 minutes or until the internal temperature of chicken reaches to 165 F.
4. Brush chicken with BBQ sauce and smoke for 10 minutes more.
5. Serve and enjoy.

Nutritional Value (Amount per Serving):

- Calories 360
- Fat 11.4 g

- Carbohydrates 17.5 g
- Sugar 13 g
- Protein 43.8 g
- Cholesterol 135 mg

Juicy Turkey Breast

Preparation Time: 10 minutes
Cooking Time: 4 hours
Serve: 4

Ingredients:

- 3 lbs turkey breast
- 4 tbsp butter, softened
- 1 ½ tbsp fresh rosemary, chopped
- 1 ½ tbsp fresh thyme, chopped
- ½ tsp pepper
- 1 tsp salt

Directions:

1. Preheat the smoker to 225F using the hickory wood chips.
2. Mix together thyme, rosemary, butter, pepper, and salt and rub all over turkey breast.
3. Place turkey breast in the smoker and smoke for 3-4 hours or until the internal temperature of turkey breast reaches to 160 F.
4. Slice and serve.

Nutritional Value (Amount per Serving):

- Calories 463
- Fat 17.5 g
- Carbohydrates 15.9 g
- Sugar 12 g
- Protein 58.4 g
- Cholesterol 177 mg

Simple Jerk Chicken

Preparation Time: 10 minutes
Cooking Time: 4 hours
Serve: 6

Ingredients:

- 5 lbs whole chicken
- 4 tbsp jerk seasoning

Directions:

1. Preheat the smoker to 275F using the applewood chips.
2. Rub jerk seasoning all over the chicken.
3. Place chicken into the smoker and smoke for 3-4 hours or until the internal temperature of chicken reaches to 160 F.
4. Slice and serve.

Nutritional Value (Amount per Serving):

- Calories 718
- Fat 28 g
- Carbohydrates 6 g
- Sugar 5.3 g
- Protein 109.4 g
- Cholesterol 336 mg

Chapter 8: Fish & Seafood

Fresh Smoked Salmon

Preparation Time: 10 minutes
Cooking Time: 60 minutes
Serve: 4

Ingredients:

- 1 ½ lbs salmon fillet
- 1 ½ tbsp Dijon mustard
- ½ tsp pepper
- 1 tsp kosher salt

Directions:

1. Preheat the smoker to 225F using the cherry wood chips.
2. Season salmon with Dijon mustard, pepper, and salt.
3. Place salmon in the smoker and cook until the internal temperature of salmon reaches to 145 F.
4. Slice and serve.

Nutritional Value (Amount per Serving):

- Calories 230
- Fat 10.7 g
- Carbohydrates 0.5 g
- Sugar 0.1 g
- Protein 33.3 g
- Cholesterol 75 mg

Cajun Shrimp

Preparation Time: 10 minutes
Cooking Time: 30 minutes
Serve: 6

Ingredients:

- 2 lbs large shrimp, cleaned
- 1 ½ tsp cayenne pepper
- 1 ½ tbsp dried thyme
- 1 ½ tbsp onion powder
- 1 lemon juice
- 1 tbsp garlic powder
- 2 ½ tbsp paprika
- Pepper
- Sea salt

Directions:

1. In a large bowl, mix together shrimp, cayenne, thyme, onion powder, garlic powder, paprika, pepper, and salt.
2. Spray foil pan with cooking spray.
3. Transfer shrimp to the foil pan and drizzle with half lemon juice.
4. Preheat the smoker to 225F using the cherry wood chips.
5. Place foil pan in the smoker and cook shrimp for 30 minutes. Stir halfway through.
6. Pour remaining lemon juice over shrimp and serve.

Nutritional Value (Amount per Serving):

- Calories 144
- Fat 0.5 g
- Carbohydrates 7.4 g
- Sugar 1.3 g
- Protein 29.3 g
- Cholesterol 216 mg

Smoked Scallops

Preparation Time: 10 minutes
Cooking Time: 40 minutes
Serve: 6

Ingredients:

- 2 lbs sea scallops, rinsed and pat dry with paper towels
- 2 garlic cloves, minced
- 2 tbsp olive oil
- 1 lemon juice
- ½ tsp pepper
- 1 tsp sea salt

Directions:

1. Preheat the smoker to 220F using the hickory wood chips.
2. Add all ingredients into the large bowl and toss well.
3. Transfer scallops mixture into the foil pan.
4. Place foil pan in the smoker and cook scallops for 35-40 minutes or until internal temperature reaches to 125 F.
5. Serve and enjoy.

Nutritional Value (Amount per Serving):

- Calories 175
- Fat 5.8 g
- Carbohydrates 4 g
- Sugar 0 g
- Protein 25.5 g
- Cholesterol 50 mg

Smoked Trout Fillets

Preparation Time: 10 minutes
Cooking Time: 2 hours
Serve: 4

Ingredients:

- 1 lb trout fillets
- 3/4 tsp fennel seeds
- 1/2 tsp mustard seeds
- 1 tbsp olive oil
- 1/2 tsp pepper
- 1 tsp kosher salt

Directions:

1. Preheat the smoker to 225F using the cherry wood chips.
2. Brush fish with oil and rub with fennel seeds, mustard seeds, pepper, and salt.
3. Place fish into the smoker and cook for 11/2-2 hours or until the internal temperature of fish fillets reaches to 125 F.
4. Serve and enjoy.

Nutritional Value (Amount per Serving):

- Calories 205
- Fat 10.3 g
- Carbohydrates 2.9 g
- Sugar 0.1 g
- Protein 25.5 g
- Cholesterol 77 mg

Smoked Salmon

Preparation Time: 10 minutes
Cooking Time: 2 hours
Serve: 6

Ingredients:

- 1 salmon fillet
- For rub:
- 1/4 cup sugar
- 1/2 cup brown sugar
- 1 1/2 tsp chili powder
- 3/4 tbsp garlic powder
- 1/2 tsp paprika
- 2 tbsp salt

Directions:

1. In a small bowl, mix together all rub ingredients and rub over salmon fillets.
2. Preheat the smoker to 225F using the applewood chips.
3. Place salmon in the smoker and cook for 2 hours.
4. Serve and enjoy.

Nutritional Value (Amount per Serving):

- Calories 122
- Fat 2 g
- Carbohydrates 21.4 g
- Sugar 20.4 g
- Protein 6.1 g
- Cholesterol 13 mg

Greek Shrimp

Preparation Time: 10 minutes
Cooking Time: 30 minutes
Serve: 6

Ingredients:

- 2 lbs shrimp, cleaned
- 1 ¼ cups feta cheese, crumbled
- ¼ cup fresh parsley, chopped
- 1 tbsp dried oregano
- 4 garlic cloves, minced
- ½ lemon juice
- 3 tbsp butter, melted
- 3 tbsp olive oil
- 1 tsp sea salt

Directions:

1. Preheat the smoker to 225F using the applewood chips.
2. Add all ingredients into the large bowl and toss well.
3. Transfer shrimp mixture into the foil pan.
4. Place foil pan in the smoker and cook for 30 minutes. Stir shrimp halfway through.
5. Serve and enjoy.

Nutritional Value (Amount per Serving):

- Calories 379
- Fat 22.1 g
- Carbohydrates 4.9 g
- Sugar 1.4 g
- Protein 39.2 g
- Cholesterol 361 mg

Lobster Tails

Preparation Time: 10 minutes
Cooking Time: 20 minutes
Serve: 4

Ingredients:

- 4 lobster tails
- 4 garlic cloves, chopped
- 4 tbsp butter, melted

Directions:

1. Preheat the smoker to 275F using the applewood chips.
2. Open lobster tails with kitchen scissors.
3. Mix together garlic and melted butter and drizzle over lobster tails.
4. Place lobster tails in the smoker and cook until internal temperature reaches to 145 F.
5. Serve and enjoy.

Nutritional Value (Amount per Serving):

- Calories 139
- Fat 11.8 g
- Carbohydrates 1.5 g
- Protein 7.3 g
- Sugar 0 g
- Cholesterol 56mg

Lemon Shrimp

Preparation Time: 10 minutes
Cooking Time: 30 minutes
Serve: 6

Ingredients:

- 2 lbs shrimp, peel and deveined
- ¼ cup fresh parsley, chopped
- 1 lemon juice
- 3 tbsp Worcestershire sauce
- ½ lb butter, melted
- 2 tbsp BBQ rub

Directions:

1. Preheat the smoker to 250F using the hickory wood chips.
2. Season shrimp with BBQ rub and place in foil pan.
3. Mix together 2 tbsp parsley, lemon juice, Worcestershire sauce, and butter and pour over shrimp.
4. Place foil pan in the smoker and cook shrimp for 25-30 minutes. Stir shrimp halfway through.
5. Garnish shrimp with remaining parsley and serve.

Nutritional Value (Amount per Serving):

- Calories 459
- Fat 33.2 g
- Carbohydrates 4 g
- Protein 34.8 g
- Sugar 1.5 g
- Cholesterol 400mg

Chapter 9: Pork

Tender & Juicy Pork Chops

Preparation Time: 10 minutes
Cooking Time: 60 minutes
Serve: 4

Ingredients:

- 4 pork chops
- 2 ½ tbsp BBQ rub
- 1 tbsp olive oil
- 1 tsp dried thyme
- 3 garlic cloves, crushed
- 1 bay leaf
- 1 ½ tsp whole peppercorns
- 1 ½ tsp fennel seeds, crushed
- 1 tsp allspice
- 3 tbsp sugar
- 7 cups of water
- 1 cup boiling water
- ¼ tsp salt

Directions:

1. Add boiling water, sugar, and salt in a large bowl and stir until sugar is dissolved.
2. Add thyme, garlic, bay leaf, peppercorns, fennel seeds, allspice, and water and stir well.
3. Now place pork chops in the bowl make sure pork chops are completely submerged in water.
4. Cover bowl and place in the refrigerator for overnight.
5. Remove pork chops from the bowl and pat dry with paper towels.

6. Preheat the smoker to 250F using the cherry wood chips.
7. Drizzle oil over pork chops and rub pork chops with BBQ spice.
8. Place pork chops in the smoker and cook for 60 minutes or until the internal temperature of pork chops reaches to 145 F.
9. Serve and enjoy.

Nutritional Value (Amount per Serving):

- Calories 285
- Fat 12 g
- Carbohydrates 10 g
- Protein 30 g
- Sugar 10 g
- Cholesterol 90mg

Perfect Baby Back Ribs

Preparation Time: 10 minutes
Cooking Time: 6 hours
Serve: 4

Ingredients:

- 3 lbs baby back ribs
- ¾ cup BBQ sauce
- ¾ cup brown sugar
- 1 cup apple juice
- 6 tbsp yellow mustard
- For rub:
- 1 tbsp onion powder
- 1 ½ tbsp Cajun seasoning
- 1 tbsp brown sugar
- 3 tbsp sugar
- 3 tbsp paprika

Directions:

1. Preheat the smoker to 225F using the applewood chips.
2. In a small bowl, mix together all rub ingredients.
3. Coat baby back ribs with mustard and rub with spice mixture.
4. Place ribs in the smoker and cook for 3 hours.
5. Add apple juice and ¾ cup brown sugar in a foil pan and mix well.
6. Remove ribs from smoker and place in foil pan. Cover foil pan with aluminum foil piece.
7. Place foil pan in the smoker and cook ribs for 2 hours.
8. Remove ribs from foil pan and brush with BBQ sauce.
9. Return ribs in the smoker and cook for 1 hour more.
10. Slice and serve.

Nutritional Value (Amount per Serving):

- Calories 528
- Fat 19.4 g
- Carbohydrates 73.8 g
- Protein 18.9 g
- Sugar 63 g
- Cholesterol 72mg

Smoked Pork Belly

Preparation Time: 10 minutes
Cooking Time: 8 hours 10 minutes
Serve: 6

Ingredients:

- 4 lbs pork belly, skinless and trimmed
- 1 1/2 tbsp paprika
- 1 1/2 tbsp chili powder
- 1/2 tsp ground mustard
- 1/2 cup brown sugar
- 1 3/4 cup BBQ sauce
- 1 1/2 tsp garlic powder
- 1 tsp onion powder
- 2 tsp kosher salt

Directions:

1. In a small bowl, mix together brown sugar, paprika, onion powder, chili powder, garlic powder, mustard, and salt and rub all over the pork belly.
2. Preheat the smoker to 225F using the applewood chips.
3. Place the pork belly in the smoker and smoke for 8 hours or until the internal temperature of the pork reaches to 190 F.
4. Brush pork belly with BBQ sauce and smoke for 10 minutes more.
5. Slice and serve.

Nutritional Value (Amount per Serving):

- Calories 453
- Fat 8.6 g
- Carbohydrates 30.9 g
- Protein 59.9 g
- Sugar 23.5 g
- Cholesterol 166 mg

Easy Pork Steaks

Preparation Time: 10 minutes
Cooking Time: 1 hour 30 minutes
Serve: 4

Ingredients:

- 4 pork steaks
- 1/2 tbsp paprika
- 1 tbsp chili powder
- 1 tsp garlic powder
- 1/2 cup brown sugar
- Pepper
- Salt

Directions:

1. In a small bowl, mix together all spices.
2. Preheat the smoker to 275F using the cherry wood chips.
3. Rub steak with spice mixture and place in the smoker and smoke for 90 minutes.
4. Slice and serve.

Nutritional Value (Amount per Serving):

- Calories 278
- Fat 11.7 g
- Carbohydrates 19.8 g
- Protein 23.1 g
- Sugar 18 g
- Cholesterol 85mg

Pulled Pork

Preparation Time: 10 minutes
Cooking Time: 8 hours 5 minutes
Serve: 8

Ingredients:

- 5 lbs pork shoulder
- 1/4 cup apple juice
- For rub:
- 3/4 tbsp garlic powder
- 2 1/2 tbsp paprika
- 3/4 tbsp dry mustard
- 1 1/2 tbsp brown sugar
- 3 tbsp sea salt
- 1 1/2 tbsp pepper

Directions:

1. Preheat the smoker to 225F using the cherry wood chips.
2. Mix together all rub ingredients and rub all over the pork shoulder.
3. Place pork shoulder in the smoker and smoke for 6 hours or until the internal temperature of the pork reaches at 160 F.
4. Remove meat from smoker and place in foil pan.
5. Pour apple juice over pork and cover the pan with foil piece.
6. Place pan in the smoker and cook until the internal temperature of the pork reaches to 190 F.
7. Shred and serve.

Nutritional Value (Amount per Serving):

- Calories 855
- Fat 61.3 g
- Carbohydrates 5.5 g

- Sugar 2.9 g
- Protein 66.9 g
- Cholesterol 255 mg

Pork Tenderloin

Preparation Time: 10 minutes
Cooking Time: 3 hours
Serve: 8

Ingredients:

- 4 lbs pork tenderloin
- 3 tbsp pork rub
- 1/2 cup apple juice
- 3 rosemary sprigs
- 3 tbsp honey
- 5 tbsp brown sugar
- 1/2 tsp pepper
- Salt

Directions:

1. In a large bowl, mix together honey, apple juice, rosemary, brown sugar, and pork rub.
2. Place meat to the bowl and coat with marinade.
3. Cover bowl and place into the refrigerator for overnight.
4. Preheat the smoker to 225F using the applewood chips.
5. Place marinated meat into the smoker and cook for 3 hours or until the internal temperature of the meat reaches to 145 F.
6. Slice and serve.

Nutritional Value (Amount per Serving):

- Calories 377
- Fat 8 g
- Carbohydrates 13.8 g
- Sugar 13.4 g
- Protein 59.4 g
- Cholesterol 166 mg

BBQ Shredded Pork

Preparation Time: 10 minutes
Cooking Time: 8 hours
Serve: 8

Ingredients:

- 4 lbs pork shoulder, boneless
- 5 tbsp BBQ rub
- 1 tbsp mustard
- 1 3/4 cups BBQ sauce
- 1 cup apple juice

Directions:

1. Preheat the smoker to 225F using the applewood chips.
2. Season meat with mustard and sprinkle with the BBQ rub.
3. Transfer meat in a foil pan and place into the smoker and smoke for 2 hours.
4. After 2 hours brush meat with apple juice.
5. Once the internal temperature of the meat reaches to 160 F then brush with remaining apple juice.
6. Cover meat with foil and turn smoker temperature to 250 F and smoke for 3-4 hours more or until the internal temperature of the meat reaches to 205 F.
7. Shred then meat using a fork and toss with BBQ sauce.
8. Serve and enjoy.

Nutritional Value (Amount per Serving):

- Calories 762
- Fat 49.1 g
- Carbohydrates 23.8 g
- Sugar 17.4 g
- Protein 53.2 g
- Cholesterol 204 mg

Honey Butter Ribs

Preparation Time: 10 minutes
Cooking Time: 4 hours
Serve: 6

Ingredients:

- 3 lbs pork side ribs
- 4 tbsp butter, melted
- 7 tbsp sriracha
- 1/2 tsp garlic powder
- ½ tsp paprika
- ½ tsp onion powder
- 1 1/2 tsp pepper
- 1/2 cup honey
- 1 tbsp salt

Directions:

1. Preheat the smoker to 275F using the hickory wood chips.
2. Spread 2 tbsp of sriracha over the ribs.
3. Place ribs in the smoker and smoke for 2 hours.
4. For the sauce: In a bowl, mix together onion powder, paprika, garlic powder, pepper, honey, butter, remaining sriracha, and salt.
5. Brush ribs with half sauce and cook for 2 hours more.
6. Remove ribs from smoker and brush with remaining sauce and smoke for 15 minutes more.
7. Serve and enjoy.

Nutritional Value (Amount per Serving):

- Calories 626
- Fat 32 g
- Carbohydrates 54 g

- Sugar 47 g
- Protein 32 g
- Cholesterol 150 mg

Easy Smoked Pork Tenderloin

Preparation Time: 10 minutes
Cooking Time: 2 hours 30 minutes
Serve: 6

Ingredients:

- 3 lbs pork tenderloin
- 1 tsp onion powder
- 2 tbsp brown sugar
- 2 tbsp harissa paste
- 1 orange juice
- 1 tsp garlic powder
- 1/2 tsp salt

Directions:

1. In a small bowl, mix together onion powder, harissa paste, garlic powder, brown sugar, and salt.
2. Spread harissa mixture over pork tenderloin evenly.
3. Preheat the smoker to 250F using the cherry wood chips.
4. Place pork tenderloin in the smoker and smoke for 2 1/2 hours or until the internal temperature of pork tenderloin reaches to 145 F.
5. Drizzle orange juice over pork tenderloin.
6. Slice and serve.

Nutritional Value (Amount per Serving):

- Calories 345
- Fat 8 g
- Carbohydrates 5 g
- Sugar 4 g
- Protein 59 g
- Cholesterol 166 mg

Delicious Pork Chops

Preparation Time: 10 minutes
Cooking Time: 2 hours
Serve: 4

Ingredients:

- 4 pork chops
- 1 tsp garlic powder
- 1/4 tsp onion powder
- 5 tbsp maple syrup
- 1/2 tsp pepper
- 1/2 tsp salt

Directions:

1. Season pork chops with onion powder, garlic powder, pepper, and salt.
2. Brush pork chops with maple syrup.
3. Preheat the smoker to 275F using the cherry wood chips.
4. Place pork chops in the smoker and smoke for 2 hours or until the internal temperature of pork chops reaches to 155 F.
5. Serve and enjoy.

Nutritional Value (Amount per Serving):

- Calories 325
- Fat 20g
- Carbohydrates 17 g
- Sugar 15 g
- Protein 18 g
- Cholesterol 69 mg

Chapter 10: Beef

Cajun Seasoned Beef Brisket

Preparation Time: 10 minutes
Cooking Time: 4 hours
Serve: 12

Ingredients:

- 10 lbs beef brisket
- For rub:
- 1 tsp Greek seasoning
- 1 tsp garlic powder
- ½ tsp paprika
- ½ tsp cayenne
- 1 tsp onion salt
- 1 ½ tbsp Cajun seasoning
- ¾ cup brown sugar
- ¼ tsp pepper
- 2 tsp salt

Directions:

1. Preheat the smoker to 250F using the hickory wood chips.
2. In a small bowl, mix together all rub ingredients and rub all over the brisket.
3. Place brisket on the middle rack of the smoker and cook for 1 hour.
4. Remove brisket from smoker and wrap in foil and smoke for 2-3 hours more or until internal temperature reaches to 180 F.
5. Slice and serve.

Nutritional Value (Amount per Serving):

- Calories 739

- Fat 23.6 g
- Carbohydrates 9.3 g
- Sugar 8.9 g
- Protein 114.8 g
- Cholesterol 338 mg

Meatloaf

Preparation Time: 10 minutes
Cooking Time: 1 hour 30 minutes
Serve: 8

Ingredients:

- 2 lb ground beef
- 1 ¾ cups cheddar cheese, shredded
- 1 medium onion, chopped
- ¾ tsp garlic powder
- 4 tbsp milk
- 1 tbsp garlic salt
- ½ cup breadcrumbs
- 2 eggs, lightly beaten
- 5 bacon slices, cooked and chopped
- ¼ tsp pepper

Directions:

1. Preheat the smoker to 325F using the applewood chips.
2. Add all ingredients into the large bowl and mix until well combined.
3. Shape meat mixture into a loaf and place in the smoker and cook for 1 ½ hour or until the internal temperature of meatloaf reaches to 165 F.
4. Slice and serve.

Nutritional Value (Amount per Serving):

- Calories 367
- Fat 16.9 g
- Carbohydrates 7.9 g
- Sugar 1.9 g
- Protein 43.5 g
- Cholesterol 169 mg

Garlic Herb Beef Roast

Preparation Time: 10 minutes
Cooking Time: 3 hours 20 minutes
Serve: 8

Ingredients:

- 6 lbs prime rib roast, bone-in
- 1 1/2 tsp rosemary, minced
- 7 tbsp butter, softened
- 2 1/2 tsp thyme, minced
- 5 garlic cloves, minced
- Pepper
- Salt

Directions:

1. Preheat the smoker to 250F using the applewood chips.
2. Mix together butter, rosemary, thyme, garlic, pepper, and salt and rub over meat.
3. Place meat in a foil pan.
4. Place pan in the smoker and smoke until the internal temperature of the meat reaches to 125 F.
5. Remove meat from the smoker and let sit for 10 minutes.
6. Slice and serve.

Nutritional Value (Amount per Serving):

- Calories 904
- Fat 70.9 g
- Carbohydrates 5 g
- Sugar 0 g
- Protein 57 g
- Cholesterol 229 mg

Chuck Roast

Preparation Time: 10 minutes
Cooking Time: 5 hours
Serve: 8

Ingredients:

- 6 lbs chuck roast
- 1 1/2 tsp garlic powder
- 1/2 tbsp onion powder
- 1 tbsp pepper
- 1 1/2 tsp old bay seasoning
- 1 tsp paprika
- 1 tbsp salt

Directions:

1. Mix together old bay seasoning, paprika, garlic powder, onion powder, pepper, and salt and rub over chuck roast.
2. Place chuck roast in refrigerator for 2-3 hours.
3. Preheat the smoker to 250F using the applewood chips.
4. Place chuck roast in the smoker and smoke for 5 hours or until the internal temperature of chuck roast reaches to 150 F.
5. Slice and serve.

Nutritional Value (Amount per Serving):

- Calories 741
- Fat 28.3 g
- Carbohydrates 1.4 g
- Sugar 0.3 g
- Protein 112 g
- Cholesterol 344 mg

Juicy Beef Ribs

Preparation Time: 10 minutes
Cooking Time: 3 hours
Serve: 4

Ingredients:

- 3 lbs beef ribs
- For rub:
- ¾ tbsp onion powder
- ½ tsp garlic powder
- 3 tbsp brown sugar
- ½ tsp pepper
- 1 tsp salt

Directions:

1. Preheat the smoker to 275F using the mesquite wood chips.
2. Mix together all rub ingredients and rub all over beef ribs.
3. Place beef ribs in the smoker and cook for 3 hours.
4. Slice and serve.

Nutritional Value (Amount per Serving):

- Calories 664
- Fat 21.2 g
- Carbohydrates 8.1 g
- Sugar 7.1 g
- Protein 103.4 g
- Cholesterol 304 mg

Meatballs

Preparation Time: 10 minutes
Cooking Time: 60 minutes
Serve: 6

Ingredients:

- 2 lbs ground beef
- 1/4 tsp pepper
- 1 tsp Italian seasoning
- 1 tsp garlic, minced
- 1 tsp onion powder
- 1/2 cup milk
- 1 1/2 bread slices, crumbled
- 1 tsp salt

Directions:

1. Add all ingredients into the mixing bowl and mix until combined.
2. Make small balls from meat mixture and place in foil pan.
3. Preheat the smoker to 250F using the cherry wood chips.
4. Place foil pan in smoker and cook meatballs for 60 minutes or until the internal temperature of meatballs reaches to 160 F.
5. Serve and enjoy.

Nutritional Value (Amount per Serving):

- Calories 302
- Fat 10.1 g
- Carbohydrates 2.8 g
- Sugar 1.2 g
- Protein 46.8 g
- Cholesterol 137 mg

Easy Beef Patties

Preparation Time: 10 minutes
Cooking Time: 30 minutes
Serve: 4

Ingredients:

- 1 lb ground beef
- 1 egg, lightly beaten
- 1 tsp chili powder
- 3/4 tsp onion powder
- 1/4 tsp garlic powder
- 1/4 tsp pepper
- Salt

Directions:

1. Preheat the smoker to 275F using the hickory wood chips.
2. In a large bowl, mix together all ingredients until combined.
3. Make patties from meat mixture.
4. Place patties in the smoker and smoke for 30 minutes or until the internal temperature of patties reach to 165 F.
5. Serve and enjoy.

Nutritional Value (Amount per Serving):

- Calories 229
- Fat 8.2 g
- Carbohydrates 0.7 g
- Sugar 0.3 g
- Protein 35.9 g
- Cholesterol 142 mg

Tip Roast

Preparation Time: 10 minutes
Cooking Time: 3 hours
Serve: 6

Ingredients:

- 2 lbs tri-tip roast
- 1/2 tsp cayenne pepper
- 1/2 tsp dried oregano
- 1/4 tsp chili powder
- 1/4 tsp onion powder
- 1/2 tsp garlic powder
- 1/2 tsp pepper
- 1 tsp salt

Directions:

1. Preheat the smoker to 275F using the applewood chips.
2. Mix together chili powder, onion powder, cayenne pepper, oregano, garlic powder, pepper, and salt and rub over roast.
3. Place roast in the smoker and smoke for 3 hours.
4. Slice and serve.

Nutritional Value (Amount per Serving):

- Calories 278
- Fat 12.7 g
- Carbohydrates 0.6 g
- Sugar 0.1 g
- Protein 40.6 g
- Cholesterol 107 mg

Flavorful Beef Tenderloin

Preparation Time: 10 minutes
Cooking Time: 25 minutes
Serve: 10

Ingredients:

- 6 lbs beef tenderloin
- 2 tsp vinegar
- 2 cups mayonnaise
- 3/4 tsp garlic powder
- 2 tsp water
- 2 garlic cloves, minced
- 1/4 tsp pepper
- 1/4 tsp kosher salt

Directions:

1. Preheat the smoker to 275F using the cherry wood chips.
2. Season beef tenderloin with garlic powder, pepper, and salt.
3. Place tenderloin in the smoker and smoke for 2 hours or until the internal temperature of tenderloin reaches to 130 F.
4. For the sauce: In a small bowl, mix together mayonnaise, garlic, vinegar, and water.
5. Slice and serve with sauce.

Nutritional Value (Amount per Serving):

- Calories 745
- Fat 40.6 g
- Carbohydrates 11.4 g
- Sugar 3.1 g
- Protein 79.3 g
- Cholesterol 263 mg

Perfect Beef Brisket

Preparation Time: 10 minutes
Cooking Time: 8 hours
Serve: 12

Ingredients:

- 10 lb beef brisket
- For rub:
- 1 tbsp ground cumin
- 1 tbsp garlic powder
- 1 tbsp onion powder
- 1 ½ tbsp paprika
- 1 tsp chili powder
- 1 tsp pepper
- 1 tbsp salt

Directions:

1. Preheat the smoker to 225 F using applewood chips.
2. Mix together all rub ingredients and rub all over the beef brisket.
3. Place beef brisket in the smoker and smoke for 8 hours or until the internal temperature of beef brisket reaches to 185 F.
4. Remove brisket from smoker and wrap in aluminum foil and let sit for 1 hour.
5. Slice and serve.

Nutritional Value (Amount per Serving):

- Calories 712
- Fat 23.9 g
- Carbohydrates 1.9 g
- Sugar 0.5 g
- Protein 115.1 g
- Cholesterol 338 mg

Chapter 11: Lamb

Leg of Lamb

Preparation Time: 10 minutes
Cooking Time: 3 hours
Serve: 4

Ingredients:

- 2 lbs leg of lamb
- 2 tbsp olive oil
- 1 tsp thyme
- 2 tbsp oregano
- 3 garlic cloves, minced
- 1 tbsp pepper
- 2 tbsp salt

Directions:

1. Mix together spices, oil, and garlic and rub all over the lamb.
2. Cover lamb with foil and place in the refrigerator for 2 hours to marinate.
3. Preheat the smoker to 250F using the oak wood chips.
4. Remove lamb from the refrigerator. Uncover and place in the smoker and smoke for 3-4 hours or until internal temperature reaches to 145 F.
5. Slice and serve.

Nutritional Value (Amount per Serving):

- Calories 497
- Fat 23.9 g
- Carbohydrates 3.4 g
- Sugar 0.1 g
- Protein 64.3 g
- Cholesterol 204 mg

Olive Wood Smoked Lamb

Preparation Time: 10 minutes
Cooking Time: 4 hours
Serve: 8

Ingredients:

- 4 ½ lbs leg of lamb
- ½ tsp coriander
- ½ tsp cumin
- 1 tsp paprika
- 1 tsp garlic powder
- 1 tsp pepper
- 1 ½ tsp salt

Directions:

1. In a small bowl, mix together coriander, cumin, paprika, garlic powder, pepper, and salt.
2. Rub spice mixture all over the lamb.
3. Preheat the smoker to 200F using the olive wood chips.
4. Place lamb in the smoker and smoke for 4 hours or until the internal temperature of lamb reaches to 142 F.
5. Slice and serve.

Nutritional Value (Amount per Serving):

- Calories 478
- Fat 18.8 g
- Carbohydrates 0.6 g
- Sugar 0.1 g
- Protein 71.8 g
- Cholesterol 230 mg

Rack of Lamb

Preparation Time: 10 minutes
Cooking Time: 2 hours
Serve: 4

Ingredients:

- 2 lbs rack of lamb
- 2 tbsp olive oil
- Pepper
- Salt
- For herb butter paste:
- 3 garlic cloves, minced
- 1 tbsp cumin
- 2 tbsp parsley, chopped
- 2 tbsp olive oil
- ¼ cup butter
- Pepper
- Salt

Directions:

1. Preheat the smoker to 225F using the hickory woods chips.
2. In a small bowl, mix together all herb butter paste ingredients.
3. Brush rack of lamb with olive oil and season with pepper and salt.
4. Coat rack of lamb with herb butter paste and place in the smoker and smoke for 2 hours or until the internal temperature of lamb reaches to 135 F.
5. Slice and serve.

Nutritional Value (Amount per Serving):

- Calories 613
- Fat 45.9 g

- Carbohydrates 1.6 g
- Sugar 0.1 g
- Protein 46.8 g
- Cholesterol 181 mg

Smoked Lamb Chops

Preparation Time: 10 minutes
Cooking Time: 45 minutes
Serve: 4

Ingredients:

- 8 lamb chops
- 1 tbsp honey
- 4 tbsp olive oil
- 2 tbsp shallots, chopped
- 2 garlic cloves, chopped
- 1 tbsp fresh thyme
- 2 tbsp fresh sage
- 2 tbsp rosemary
- ½ tsp pepper
- ½ tsp salt

Directions:

1. Preheat the smoker to 225F using the applewood chips.
2. Add all ingredients except lamb chops into the food processor and process until smooth.
3. Coat lamb chops with herb paste and place in the smoker and smoke for 45 minutes or until the internal temperature of lamb reaches to 120 F.
4. Serve and enjoy.

Nutritional Value (Amount per Serving):

- Calories 218
- Fat 18.2 g
- Carbohydrates 9.2 g
- Sugar 4.4 g
- Protein 6.8 g
- Cholesterol 0 mg

Dijon Rack of Lambs

Preparation Time: 10 minutes
Cooking Time: 1 hour 30 minutes
Serve: 4

Ingredients:

- 1 rack of lamb
- For marinade:
- 3 garlic cloves, crushed
- ½ tsp pepper
- 1 tsp dried rosemary
- 2 tbsp Dijon mustard
- ¼ cup olive oil
- 2 tbsp fresh lemon juice
- For rub:
- ¼ cup olive oil
- 1 tsp dried parsley
- 1 tsp dried basil
- 1 tsp dried rosemary
- 1 tsp dried mint
- 1 tsp dried oregano
- ¼ tsp cayenne pepper
- 1 tsp onion powder
- 1 tsp garlic powder
- 1 tbsp Dijon mustard
- Salt

Directions:

1. Add marinade ingredients into the large zip-lock bag and mix well.

2. Add rack of lamb to the zip-lock bag and coat well with marinade and place in the refrigerator for 2-3 hours.
3. Remove rack of lamb from marinade and brush with 1 tbsp mustard and season with cayenne, onion powder, and garlic.
4. Mix together herb and rub onto lamb. Drizzle with olive oil.
5. Preheat the smoker to 225F using the applewood chips.
6. Place the rack of lamb in the smoker and smoke for 1 ½ hour or until the internal temperature of lamb reaches to 145 F.
7. Slice and serve.

Nutritional Value (Amount per Serving):

- Calories 455
- Fat 43 g
- Carbohydrates 14 g
- Sugar 7 g
- Protein 7 g
- Cholesterol 12 mg

Smoked Leg of Lamb

Preparation Time: 10 minutes
Cooking Time: 4 hours
Serve: 8

Ingredients:

- 1 leg of lamb, bone-in
- 2 tbsp mustard
- For rub:
- ½ tsp paprika
- 1 tsp brown sugar
- 1 tsp rosemary
- 1 tsp thyme
- 1 tsp granulated garlic
- 2 tsp pepper
- 1 tsp kosher salt

Directions:

1. In a small bowl, mix together paprika, sugar, rosemary, thyme, garlic, pepper, and salt.
2. Rub mustard over the lamb and season lamb with spice mixture.
3. Preheat the smoker to 250F using the cherry wood chips.
4. Place lamb in the smoker and smoke for 4 hours or until internal temperature reaches to 150 F.
5. Slice and serve.

Nutritional Value (Amount per Serving):

- Calories 651
- Fat 25.8 g
- Carbohydrates 2.2 g
- Sugar 0.7 g
- Protein 96.4 g
- Cholesterol 306 mg

Delicious Lamb Rack

Preparation Time: 10 minutes
Cooking Time: 45 minutes
Serve: 2

Ingredients:

- 1 lb lamb rack
- 2 tsp celery salt
- 2 tsp garlic powder
- ¼ tsp cayenne pepper
- 2 tsp sweet paprika
- 1 tbsp kosher salt
- 1 tbsp pepper
- 1 tbsp dried rosemary

Directions:

1. In a small bowl, mix together rosemary, pepper, salt, paprika, cayenne, garlic powder, and celery salt.
2. Coat lamb rack evenly with rosemary mixture and place in the refrigerator for overnight.
3. Preheat the smoker to 250F using the applewood chips.
4. Place marinated lamb rack in the smoker and smoke for 45 minutes or until internal temperature reaches to 140 F.
5. Slice and serve.

Nutritional Value (Amount per Serving):

- Calories 452
- Fat 17.3 g
- Carbohydrates 6.6 g
- Sugar 1 g
- Protein 65 g
- Cholesterol 204 mg

BBQ Smoked Lamb

Preparation Time: 10 minutes
Cooking Time: 3 hours
Serve: 4

Ingredients:

- 2 lbs leg of lamb
- ½ cup BBQ sauce

Directions:

1. Preheat the smoker to 250F using the applewood chips.
2. Brush lamb with BBQ sauce and place in the smoker and smoke for 3 hours or until internal temperature reaches to 165 F.
3. Slice and serve.

Nutritional Value (Amount per Serving):

- Calories 469
- Fat 16.7 g
- Carbohydrates 11.3 g
- Sugar 8.1 g
- Protein 63.7 g
- Cholesterol 204 mg

Garlickey Leg of Lamb

Preparation Time: 10 minutes
Cooking Time: 2 hours
Serve: 8

Ingredients:

- 2 lbs leg of lamb
- 4 tbsp olive oil
- 3 tbsp rosemary, chopped
- 1 lemon zest
- 1 lemon juice
- 5 garlic cloves, crushed
- 1 tbsp pepper
- 2 tbsp sea salt

Directions:

1. Preheat the smoker to 250F using the applewood chips.
2. In a small bowl, mix together garlic, oil, rosemary, lemon juice, lemon zest, pepper, and salt.
3. Rub garlic mixture over the lamb and place lamb in the smoker and smoke for 2 hours or until the internal temperature of lamb reaches to 145 F.
4. Slice and serve.

Nutritional Value (Amount per Serving):

- Calories 280
- Fat 15.5 g
- Carbohydrates 1.9 g
- Sugar 0 g
- Protein 32.1 g
- Cholesterol 102 mg

Indian Spiced Lamb

Preparation Time: 10 minutes
Cooking Time: 2 hours
Serve: 6

Ingredients:

- 5 lbs leg of lamb
- For the spice paste:
- ½ tsp turmeric powder
- 1 tsp chili powder
- 1 tsp cinnamon
- 1 tsp ground coriander
- 1 tsp paprika
- 3 garlic cloves, minced
- 2 tsp ground cumin
- 1 tsp sea salt
- 1 tsp ginger, grated
- 1 tbsp lemon juice
- 1/3 cup yogurt

Directions:

1. Preheat the smoker to 250F using the hickory wood chips.
2. Mix together all spice paste ingredients and rub all over the lamb.
3. Place lamb in the smoker and smoke until the internal temperature of lamb reaches to 145 F, about 2 hours.
4. Slice and serve.

Nutritional Value (Amount per Serving):

- Calories 723
- Fat 28.2 g

- Carbohydrates 2.9 g
- Sugar 1.2 g
- Protein 107.3 g
- Cholesterol 341 mg

Chapter 12: Game Recipes

Easy Smoked Cornish Hens

Preparation Time: 10 minutes
Cooking Time: 60 minutes
Serve: 6

Ingredients:

- 6 cornish hens, trimmed and giblets removed
- 6 tbsp BBQ rub
- 2 tbsp olive oil

Directions:

1. Preheat the smoker to 275F using the applewood chips.
2. Brush hens with oil and coat with BBQ rub.
3. Place hens in the smoker and cook for 30 minutes.
4. Turn hens to other side and cook for 30 minutes more or until internal temperature reaches to 165 F.
5. Slice and serve.

Nutritional Value (Amount per Serving):

- Calories 335
- Fat 13.2 g
- Carbohydrates 0 g
- Sugar 0 g
- Protein 51.3 g
- Cholesterol 233 mg

Flavorful Cornish Hen

Preparation Time: 10 minutes
Cooking Time: 2 hours 30 minutes
Serve: 2

Ingredients:

- 2 cornish hens
- For rub:
- 1 tsp ground thyme
- 3/4 tbsp onion powder
- ¾ tbsp paprika
- ½ tsp sage
- Pepper
- Salt

Directions:

1. In a small bowl, mix together all rub ingredients and rub all over the Cornish hens.
2. Preheat the smoker to 175F using the applewood chips.
3. Place Cornish hens in the smoker and smoke until the internal temperature of hens reaches to 185 F.
4. Slice and serve.

Nutritional Value (Amount per Serving):

- Calories 313
- Fat 8.9 g
- Carbohydrates 4 g
- Sugar 1.2 g
- Protein 52 g
- Cholesterol 233 mg

Orange Glazed Cornish Hens

Preparation Time: 10 minutes
Cooking Time: 2 hours
Serve: 2

Ingredients:

- 2 cornish hens
- 4 garlic cloves
- 8 fresh sage leaves
- 3 fresh rosemary sprigs
- ½ onion, cut into chunks
- ½ orange cut into wedges
- For glaze:
- 1 orange zest
- 3 oz grand Marnier
- 1 cinnamon stick
- 4-star anise
- 2 tbsp honey
- 2 cups orange juice
- ½ fresh orange, sliced

Directions:

1. Stuff each hen with half of the orange wedges, garlic, onions, and herbs. Season with pepper and salt.
2. Preheat the smoker to 175F using the hickory wood chips.
3. Place hens in the smoker and smoke for 1 ½-2 hour or until the internal temperature of hens reach to 165 F.
4. Meanwhile, in a saucepan heat, all glaze ingredients until reduce by half over medium-high heat.
5. Remove hens from smoker and brush with glaze.

6. Slice and serve.

Nutritional Value (Amount per Serving):

- Calories 425
- Fat 5.6 g
- Carbohydrates 80 g
- Sugar 56 g
- Protein 12.9 g
- Cholesterol 21 mg

Herb Butter Cornish Hens

Preparation Time: 10 minutes
Cooking Time: 2 hours
Serve: 4

Ingredients:

- 4 cornish hens, rinse and pat dry with paper towels
- 4 tsp poultry seasoning
- 4 tbsp butter, melted
- 4 rosemary sprigs

Directions:

1. Stuff rosemary sprigs into the hen's cavity.
2. Brush hens with melted butter and season with poultry seasoning.
3. Preheat the smoker to 225F using the hickory wood chips.
4. Place hens in the smoker and smoke for 1-2 hours or until the internal temperature of hens reaches to 165 F.
5. Slice and serve.

Nutritional Value (Amount per Serving):

- Calories 401
- Fat 20.1 g
- Carbohydrates 1 g
- Sugar 0.1 g
- Protein 51.5 g
- Cholesterol 265 mg

Orange Stuff Cornish Hens

Preparation Time: 10 minutes
Cooking Time: 2 hours 30 minutes
Serve: 4

Ingredients:

- 4 cornish hens, rinsed and pat dry with paper towels
- 2 tsp dried thyme
- 4 oranges, cut into quarters
- ¼ cup olive oil
- Pepper
- Salt

Directions:

1. Preheat the smoker to 250F using the hickory wood chips.
2. Stuff hens cavity with orange quarters.
3. Bush hens with oil and season with thyme, pepper, and salt.
4. Place hens in the smoker and smoke for 2 ½ hours or until the internal temperature of hens reaches to 165 F.
5. Remove hens from the smoker and let sit for 15 minutes.
6. Slice and serve.

Nutritional Value (Amount per Serving):

- Calories 491
- Fat 21.4 g
- Carbohydrates 22 g
- Sugar 17.2 g
- Protein 53 g
- Cholesterol 233 mg

Herbed Cornish Hens

Preparation Time: 10 minutes
Cooking Time: 2 hours 30 minutes
Serve: 4

Ingredients:

- 4 cornish hens, thawed and remove giblets
- ½ tsp dried sage
- ½ tsp dried rosemary
- 3 garlic cloves, minced
- 1 tbsp dry sherry
- 3 tbsp butter, melted

Directions:

1. Preheat the smoker to 250F using the applewood chips.
2. Mix together butter, sherry, garlic, rosemary, and sage and rub over the hens.
3. Place hens in the smoker and smoke hens until the internal temperature of hens reaches to 165 F, about 2 ½ hours.
4. Slice and serve.

Nutritional Value (Amount per Serving):

- Calories 375
- Fat 17.2 g
- Carbohydrates 0.9 g
- Sugar 0 g
- Protein 51.5 g
- Cholesterol 256 mg

Delicious Cornish Game Hens

Preparation Time: 10 minutes
Cooking Time: 2 hours
Serve: 2

Ingredients:

- 2 cornish hens, rinsed and pat dry with paper towels
- ¾ tsp cayenne
- 1 tsp thyme
- 1 tsp oregano
- 1 ½ tbsp basil
- 2 tbsp butter, melted
- 1 tsp chili powder
- 1 tsp pepper
- 1 tbsp salt

Directions:

1. Brush hens with butter. Mix together basil, oregano, thyme, cayenne, chili powder, pepper, and salt and rub all over the hens.
2. Preheat the smoker to 275F using the hickory wood chips.
3. Place hens in the smoker and cook until the internal temperature of hens reaches to 180 F, about 2 hours.
4. Slice and serve.

Nutritional Value (Amount per Serving):

- Calories 410
- Fat 20.5 g
- Carbohydrates 2.6 g
- Sugar 0.2 g
- Protein 51.9 g
- Cholesterol 265 mg

Smoked Vension Tenderloins

Preparation Time: 10 minutes
Cooking Time: 2 hours
Serve: 4

Ingredients:

- 12 oz venison tenderloins, trimmed
- 1 tsp dried rosemary
- 3 garlic cloves, minced
- ½ small onion, diced
- 1 tsp honey
- 1 tsp Dijon mustard
- 1 tbsp soy sauce
- ¼ cup olive oil
- 1/3 dry red wine
- 1 tsp pepper
- 1 tsp sea salt

Directions:

1. Add all ingredients except meat into the large zip-lock bag and mix well.
2. Now add meat into the zip-lock bag and coat well with marinade. Seal bag and place in the refrigerator for overnight.
3. Preheat the smoker to 250F using the applewood chips
4. Remove meat from marinade and place in the smoker and smoke for 2 hours or until the internal temperature of the meat reaches to 150 F.
5. Remove meat from the smoker and let sit for 10 minutes.
6. Slice and serve.

Nutritional Value (Amount per Serving):

- Calories 281
- Fat 18.7 g

- Carbohydrates 3.9 g
- Sugar 1.9 g
- Protein 21.6 g
- Cholesterol 81 mg

BBQ Cornish Hens

Preparation Time: 10 minutes
Cooking Time: 1 hour 30 minutes
Serve: 8

Ingredients:

- 4 cornish hens
- ½ cup BBQ rub

Directions:

1. Preheat the smoker to 250F using the hickory wood chips.
2. Coat hens with BBQ rub and place in the smoker and smoke for 1 ½ hour or until the internal temperature of hens reaches to 165 F.
3. Remove hens from the smoker and let sit for 10 minutes.
4. Slice and serve.

Nutritional Value (Amount per Serving):

- Calories 147
- Fat 4.3 g
- Carbohydrates 0 g
- Sugar 0 g
- Protein 25.6 g
- Cholesterol 117 mg

Asian Smoked Cornish Hen

Preparation Time: 10 minutes
Cooking Time: 3 hours
Serve: 2

Ingredients:

- 1 cornish hen
- 2 cups of water
- 3 tbsp soy sauce
- 2 tbsp sugar
- 1 ½ tsp Chinese five-spice powder
- 1 ½ tsp rice wine
- ½ tsp pepper
- Salt

Directions:

1. In a large bowl, mix together water, soy sauce, sugar, rice wine, five-spice, pepper, and salt.
2. Place Cornish hen in the bowl and place in the refrigerator for overnight.
3. Preheat the smoker to 225F using the applewood chips.
4. Remove Cornish hen from marinade and place in the smoker and smoke for 3 hours.
5. Slice and serve.

Nutritional Value (Amount per Serving):

- Calories 213
- Fat 4.3 g
- Carbohydrates 15.9 g
- Sugar 13.4 g
- Protein 27.2 g
- Cholesterol 117 mg

Simple Smoked Cornish Hens

Preparation Time: 10 minutes
Cooking Time: 2 hours
Serve: 2

Ingredients:

- 2 cornish hens
- 2 tsp pepper
- 1-gallon water
- 1 cup kosher salt

Directions:

1. For the brine: Add water, salt, and pepper in a large pot and stir until salt dissolved.
2. Add hens into the brine and place in the refrigerator for 4 hours.
3. Preheat the smoker to 225F using the hickory wood chips.
4. Remove hens from brine and place in the smoker and smoke for 2 hours or until the internal temperature of hens reaches to 165 F.
5. Slice and serve.

Nutritional Value (Amount per Serving):

- Calories 300
- Fat 8.6 g
- Carbohydrates 1.4 g
- Sugar 0 g
- Protein 51.5 g
- Cholesterol 230 mg

Easy & Flavorful Cornish Hens

Preparation Time: 10 minutes
Cooking Time: 1 hour 30 minutes
Serve: 4

Ingredients:

- 4 cornish hens
- 4 cinnamon sticks
- 4 cups hot water
- 4 cups cold water
- 64 oz apple juice
- ½ cup brown sugar
- 1 cup kosher salt

Directions:

1. Add cinnamon, hot water, cold water, apple juice, brown sugar, and salt into the large pot and stir until sugar is dissolved.
2. Add hens in the brine and place in the refrigerator for 5-6 hours.
3. Preheat the smoker to 250F using the cherry wood chips.
4. Remove hens from brine and place in the smoker and smoke for 1 ½ hour or until internal temperature reaches to 160 F.
5. Remove hens from the smoker and let sit for 10 minutes.
6. Slice and serve.

Nutritional Value (Amount per Serving):

- Calories 147
- Fat 4.3 g
- Carbohydrates 0 g
- Sugar 0 g
- Protein 25.6 g
- Cholesterol 117 mg

Chapter 13: Sides

Smoked Olives & Cherry Tomatoes

Preparation Time: 10 minutes
Cooking Time: 60 minutes
Serve: 6

Ingredients:

- 1 cup olives, pitted
- 4 cups cherry tomatoes
- ½ tsp pepper
- 1 tsp olive oil
- ½ tsp salt

Directions:

1. Preheat the smoker to 225F using the cherry wood chips.
2. Add cherry tomatoes in the foil pan and season with pepper and salt. Drizzle with olive oil.
3. Place foil pan in the smoker and cook for 45-60 minutes.
4. Remove foil pan from smoker. Add olives and stir well.
5. Serve and enjoy.

Nutritional Value (Amount per Serving):

- Calories 54
- Fat 3.4 g
- Carbohydrates 6.2 g
- Sugar 3.2 g
- Protein 1.3 g
- Cholesterol 0 mg

Smoked Shrimp Skewers

Preparation Time: 10 minutes
Cooking Time: 30 minutes
Serve: 6

Ingredients:

- 1 1/2 lbs jumbo shrimp
- 4 garlic cloves, chopped
- 1/2 cup olive oil
- 1/2 tsp pepper
- 1 tsp cayenne pepper
- 2 tbsp fresh parsley, chopped
- 1/2 tsp salt

Directions:

1. Add shrimp in a large bowl with remaining ingredients and toss well.
2. Thread shrimp onto the skewers.
3. Preheat the smoker to 225F using the cherry wood chips.
4. Place shrimp skewers in the smoker and smoke for 30 minutes.
5. Serve and enjoy.

Nutritional Value (Amount per Serving):

- Calories 230
- Fat 16.9 g
- Carbohydrates 1 g
- Sugar 2.1 g
- Protein 20.5 g
- Cholesterol 233 mg

Beef Bites

Preparation Time: 10 minutes
Cooking Time: 3 hours
Serve: 8

Ingredients:

- 3 lbs beef roast, trim and cut into 1-inch pieces
- 2 1/2 tbsp soy sauce
- 3/4 cup teriyaki sauce
- 3 tbsp olive oil
- 5 tbsp honey
- 1 1/2 tsp red chili flakes

Directions:

1. In a large bowl, mix together oil, chili flakes, soy sauce, teriyaki sauce, and honey.
2. Add meat in the bowl and coat well with marinade.
3. Cover bowl and place in the refrigerator for overnight.
4. Preheat the smoker to 225F using the hickory wood chips.
5. Place marinated beef cubes into the smoker and smoke for 2-3 hours.
6. Serve and enjoy.

Nutritional Value (Amount per Serving):

- Calories 428
- Fat 15.9 g
- Carbohydrates 15.4 g
- Sugar 14.7 g
- Protein 53.6 g
- Cholesterol 152 mg

Smoked Green Beans

Preparation Time: 10 minutes
Cooking Time: 60 minutes
Serve: 4

Ingredients:

- 24 oz green beans, ends trimmed
- ½ butter, melted
- Pepper
- Salt

Directions:

1. Arrange green beans to the foil pan and drizzle with butter.
2. Season green beans with pepper and salt.
3. Preheat the smoker to 275F using the applewood chips.
4. Place green beans in the smoker and smoke for 60 minutes or until beans are tender.
5. Serve and enjoy.

Nutritional Value (Amount per Serving):

- Calories 256
- Fat 23.2 g
- Carbohydrates 12.2 g
- Sugar 2.4 g
- Protein 3.3 g
- Cholesterol 61 mg

Sweet & Smoky Ketchup

Preparation Time: 10 minutes
Cooking Time: 2 hours
Serve: 12

Ingredients:

- 2 cups ketchup
- 1/8 tsp paprika
- ¼ tsp garlic powder
- ½ tbsp hot sauce
- 2 tbsp molasses

Directions:

1. Preheat the smoker to 250 F with cherry wood chips.
2. Add all ingredients in a bowl and whisk until smooth.
3. Transfer bowl mixture to a foil pie pan.
4. Place pan in the smoker and smoke for 2 hours. Stir after 1 hour.
5. Stir and serve.

Nutritional Value (Amount per Serving):

- Calories 55
- Fat 1 g
- Carbohydrates 12 g
- Sugar 11 g
- Protein 1 g
- Cholesterol 55 mg

Baked Beans

Preparation Time: 10 minutes
Cooking Time: 2 hours
Serve: 10

Ingredients:

- 50 oz can pork & beans
- 1 pack bacon, chopped
- 2 tbsp mustard
- 1 small onion, chopped
- ¼ cup molasses
- ¼ cup brown sugar

Directions:

1. Add all ingredients except bacon into the large bowl and mix until well combined.
2. Pour bean mixture into a foil pan and top with bacon.
3. Preheat the smoker to 225F using the applewood chips.
4. Place pan in the smoker and smoke beans for 2 hours.
5. Serve and enjoy.

Nutritional Value (Amount per Serving):

- Calories 360
- Fat 13 g
- Carbohydrates 42 g
- Sugar 10 g
- Protein 18 g
- Cholesterol 49 mg

Smoked Mac & Cheese

Preparation Time: 10 minutes
Cooking Time: 1 hour 30 minutes
Serve: 10

Ingredients:

- 1 lb elbow macaroni noodles
- 1 stick butter
- 1 cup milk
- 1 lb Velveeta cheese, cubed
- Pepper
- Salt

Directions:

1. Cook macaroni according to the packet directions and drain well.
2. Add cooked macaroni, butter, milk, and cheese in a large pot and cook over medium heat until cheese is melted.
3. Preheat the smoker to 225F using the applewood chips.
4. Pour macaroni mixture in a foil pan and place in the smoker and cook for 1 ½ hour.
5. Serve and enjoy.

Nutritional Value (Amount per Serving):

- Calories 355
- Fat 16 g
- Carbohydrates 40 g
- Sugar 5 g
- Protein 13 g
- Cholesterol 45 mg

Smoked Asparagus

Preparation Time: 10 minutes
Cooking Time: 60 minutes
Serve: 4

Ingredients:

- 1 lb fresh asparagus, cut the ends
- 2 tsp olive oil
- Pepper
- Salt

Directions:

1. Preheat the smoker to 225F using the applewood chips.
2. Arrange asparagus in a foil pan and drizzle with olive oil. Season with pepper and salt.
3. Place foil pan in the smoker and smoke for 1 hour. Turn asparagus halfway through.
4. Serve and enjoy.

Nutritional Value (Amount per Serving):

- Calories 43
- Fat 2.5 g
- Carbohydrates 4.4 g
- Sugar 2.1 g
- Protein 2.5 g
- Cholesterol 0 mg

Simple Smoked Scallops

Preparation Time: 10 minutes
Cooking Time: 20 minutes
Serve: 6

Ingredients:

- 2 lbs scallops
- Pepper
- Salt

Directions:

1. Preheat the smoker to 225F using the applewood chips.
2. Season scallops using the pepper and salt.
3. Place scallops into the smoker and smoke for 20 minutes.
4. Serve and enjoy.

Nutritional Value (Amount per Serving):

- Calories 133
- Fat 1.2 g
- Carbohydrates 3.6 g
- Sugar 0 g
- Protein 25.4 g
- Cholesterol 50 mg

Smoked Italian Meatballs

Preparation Time: 10 minutes
Cooking Time: 2 hours
Serve: 4

Ingredients:

- 1/2 lb ground pork
- 1/4 tsp cayenne pepper
- 1 tbsp fresh thyme, chopped
- 1 egg, lightly beaten
- 1/2 onion, diced
- 1/4 cup breadcrumbs
- 1 tbsp fresh basil, chopped
- 2 tbsp fresh parsley, chopped

Directions:

1. Preheat the smoker to 225F using the cherry wood chips.
2. In a large bowl, mix together all ingredients until well combined.
3. Make balls from meat mixture and place in foil pan.
4. Place foil pan in smoker and smoke for 1-2 hours or until the internal temperature of meatballs reaches to 165 F.
5. Serve and enjoy.

Nutritional Value (Amount per Serving):

- Calories 132
- Fat 3.5 g
- Carbohydrates 6.9 g
- Sugar 1.1 g
- Protein 17.4 g
- Cholesterol 82 mg

Conclusion

In this book we have to introduce one of the most interesting cooking methods knows as smoking food. Smoking food is one of the traditional methods to cook food with smoke. In this book, we have to learn about Masterbuilt electric smoker. This step by step guide helps you to know more about Masterbuilt electric smoker from its history to make a delicious recipe. Using this book, you can easily understand the various benefits of the electric smoker with some useful tips and tricks.

In this book, you will get 75 delicious Masterbuilt smoker recipes that are easy to prepare.

Made in the
USA
Monee, IL